ELIZABETH COLEMAN first came to attention with her dark comedy *It's My Party (And I'll Die If I Want To)* which premiered at the 1993 Melbourne Comedy Festival and has been regularly produced ever since. In 1999 Elizabeth's next play, *Secret Bridesmaids' Business*, broke box office records in Melbourne before embarking on a triumphant national tour in 2000 and being adapted into a telemovie, produced by Linda House for ABC Television. *Secret Bridesmaids' Business* has also been produced many times, including a musical production in Tokyo by Takarazuka Creative Arts. Elizabeth's comedy about love gone wrong, *This Way Up*, premiered in Melbourne in 2001. Elizabeth has also written many screenplays for television, most recently 'Miss Fisher's Murder Mysteries'. She co-created and co-wrote the popular drama series 'Bed of Roses', with Jutta Goetze, for Southern Star and ABC Television. *Almost with You* premiered at Melbourne's La Mama Theatre in 2012.

For June, Marianne, Jackie,
Stephanie and David

Elizabeth Coleman

Almost with you

CURRENCY PRESS
SYDNEY

CURRENCY PLAYS

First published in 2014
by Currency Press Pty Ltd,
PO Box 2287, Strawberry Hills, NSW, 2012, Australia
enquiries@currency.com.au
www.currency.com.au

Copyright: *Almost with You* © Elizabeth Coleman, 2014.

Cataloguing-in-publication data for this title is available from the National Library of Australia website: www.nla.gov.au

Typeset by Dean Nottle for Currency Press.
Cover photograph by Sally Baillieu.
Cover design by Katy Wall.

Currency Press acknowledges the Traditional Owners of the Country on which we live and work. We pay our respects to all Aboriginal and Torres Strait Islander Elders, past and present.

Almost with You was first produced by The Little Theatre Company at La Mama Theatre, Melbourne, on 4 July 2012, with the following cast:

LISA FITZGERALD	Fiona Macleod
TOM FLANNERY	Raj Sidhu
DAN FITZGERALD	Luke O'Sullivan
JENNIFER BENNETT	Helen Hopkins

Director, Kaarin Fairfax
Designer, Virginia Dowzer
Lighting Designer, Stelios Karagiannis
Producer, Sally Baillieu

CHARACTERS

LISA FITZGERALD, journalist, 45
TOM FLANNERY, accountant, 50
DANIEL (DAN) FITZGERALD, courier van driver, 20
JENNIFER BENNETT, lawyer and new mother, 46
BARBARA FITZGERALD, various ages
MALE DOCTOR, 50ish

There is also a baby:
Ivy Bennett, 2 months

The actor playing Tom will double as Male Doctor.
The actor playing Jennifer will double as Barbara Fitzgerald.

SETTING

The setting is inner-suburban Melbourne, Australia. The year is primarily 2007, but New Wave music from the early 1980s is an essential part of our story.

NOTES

Almost with You unfolds fluidly over several different locations and timeframes. The locations are suggested by minimal props, except for Dan's bedroom which is cluttered with vinyl LPs, *New Musical Express* magazines, clothes, shoes, band posters and general young male detritus, all of which dates back to 1982.

Transitions are aided by sound effects and lighting design, and dates appear on a screen above the stage to help transitions into flashbacks. This screen will also double as Lisa's computer monitor.

Although scene changes are indicated by ◊ ◊ ◊ , there is no break in the action between scenes except where music is used to help change gears or to deepen an emotional point.

In the darkness we hear the song 'Alone with You' by The Sunnyboys (1981).

A date appears on a screen above the stage: '2007'.

Lights fade up. LISA *(45) and* TOM *(50) are sitting on Tom's couch in lamplight, kissing. They're fully clothed.* LISA *is straddling* TOM'*s lap.*

As 'Alone with You' fades TOM *pulls* LISA *closer, but she starts wincing.*

LISA: Ooh… Umm, I just… Sorry, I have to…

> *She pulls away.*

TOM: Lisa? Sorry. Was I being too…?

LISA: No, it's my knees.

> *She's torn between embarrassment and amusement as she climbs off his lap and sits beside him, stretching her legs.*

They're not what they used to be.

TOM: [*smiling*] Are you okay?

LISA: I'm fine—I've just got under-developed adductor muscles, according to my Pilates teacher.

TOM: I didn't know that you did Pilates.

LISA: I don't do it very well.

> *They laugh.*

I shouldn't say that, it's not a competitive sport… Have you ever noticed how before forty your physical ailments just go away? But after forty they hang around and become a management issue?

TOM: That's so true.

> *He smiles at her shyly. She leans in and kisses him. They start up again.*

[*Murmuring*] I've got a prolapsed disc.

LISA: A prolapsed what?

TOM: Disc. With an 's'. In my lower back.

LISA: [*laughing*] Oh… you poor thing…

TOM: I moved the fridge the wrong way one day and I just felt my back slip out.

LISA: Ouch.

TOM: Yeah. It comes and goes.

LISA: Do *you* do Pilates?

TOM: No, but people keep telling me I should.

LISA: They're probably right.

TOM: So you like Pilates?

LISA: I like leaving Pilates. I'm not mad about it when I'm actually there, but I can feel it doing me good.

TOM: I should think about it. When Grace says, 'Daddy, hang me upside down!', I have to say, 'Sorry, sweetie, don't forget Daddy's bad back'.

LISA: Oh… Well, at least it doesn't stop you from giving her a cuddle.

TOM: No, but I think she'd beat me in an arm wrestle.

> LISA *laughs.* TOM *leans over and gently guides her onto her back. He climbs on top of her.* LISA *is self-conscious about her middle-aged body.*

LISA: Could you turn out the light?

> TOM *switches off the lamp. We see their shapes in the darkness as they kiss. Seconds pass.*

TOM: [*in the darkness*] You know, you could claim your Pilates as a deduction.

LISA: [*in the darkness*] Could I?

TOM: [*in the darkness*] I shouldn't bring up tax.

LISA: [*in the darkness*] No, it's okay. Could I really?

TOM: [*in the darkness*] Absolutely. You're a journalist. You spend most of your time at a computer—that messes with your neck and shoulder muscles.

LISA: [*in the darkness*] I should have thought of that.

TOM: [*in the darkness*] That's *my* job. Why don't you bring it—?

LISA: [*interrupting*] Shit. Tom, there's something under…

> TOM *turns on the light.* LISA *reaches under her bum and pulls out a pair of reading glasses with a crooked arm.*

Oh no, it's glasses! I'm sorry. I didn't see them.

TOM: Don't worry, that arm's always been wonky.

LISA: Weally?

TOM: Yes, weally. Why don't you bring me your Pilates receipts? You need deductions because you don't have dependents.

LISA: Which reminds me, I'm supposed to be interviewing you about your dependents… which I guess makes this another deduction.

TOM: What? This?

He kisses her.

LISA: [*laughing*] No, not this. Dinner. You know what I mean.

She sits up and looks at him from a different angle. Her tone changes, she's now in journalist mode.

So. How did it feel, becoming a father for the first time at forty-seven? What was your overwhelming emotion?

TOM: Exhaustion.

LISA: I bet, but what else?

TOM: Well… joy obviously, but I was shit-scared too… terrified of what could happen but filled with love for this tiny person… I'm not very good at explaining it.

LISA: You did okay.

TOM: I had an hour alone with Grace while Sue was in Recovery, and I remember thinking, 'So *this* is how a father feels. If anyone hurt her, I think I'd kill them.' And when they brought Sue into the ward, I didn't want to hand her over.

LISA: You must miss her a lot.

TOM: It was Sue's decision, what can I do? You can't force someone to be with you.

LISA: But no regrets?

TOM: About Grace? Are you kidding?

LISA: [*smiling*] That was the dumbest question I've asked in a while.

TOM: What made you decide to write about older parents?

LISA: Truthfully? I didn't. It was a colleague's story, but she had to pull out… And it's in the zeitgeist, that's for sure. My best friend Jenny just had her first baby… a little girl, Ivy.

TOM: Ivy? That was on our list.

LISA: She's gorgeous, but my God, it's relentless.

She mock shudders.

TOM: Not for you, then?

LISA: My pet rock doesn't poo its nappies.

TOM: [*laughing*] Your pet rock... We've got a pet schnauzer. Colonel Klink.

LISA: Colonel Klink? What a great name for a schnauzer! Isn't it weird that we've known each other for ten years but I didn't know you had a schnauzer called Colonel Klink?

TOM: I love that dog. I miss him almost as much as I miss Grace. Does that sound crazy?

LISA: Not to me. I had a labradoodle called Daisy. She was black with a white chest, she was *so* gorgeous... But when she was six she choked on some chicken bones my father gave her—it wasn't Dad's fault, he didn't realise—but it was so horrendous.

TOM: That's horrible.

LISA: Yeah... it was five years ago.

TOM: Did you get another dog?

LISA: No. My pet rock doesn't need walking. It's a win-win.

> TOM *puts his arm around her. She nestles into him. A comfortable silence.*

TOM: I'd forgotten all about pet rocks... When were they in? The eighties?

LISA: Yeah. I knew if I kept it long enough, it'd come back into fashion.

TOM: It's all cyclical, isn't it?

LISA: Yeah. A girl in a shop—she looked about twelve—tried to sell me a poncho the other day. I said, 'No thanks, I was there the first time'.

TOM: Music's the same. Vinyl's cool again.

LISA: Yeah, I know.

TOM: My nephew collects vinyl records. He DJs—takes bits from this, bits from the other. He's into The Jam, Joy Division, The Clash—

LISA: Really?

TOM: Yeah. The Clash *and* 'doof doof' music—from the sublime to the ridiculous, eh?

> LISA *makes a spur of the moment decision.*

LISA: You know what? I've got lots of vinyl records—The Jam, The Clash, Stiff Little Fingers, The Sunnyboys—he could have them.

TOM: Really?

The smallest hint of hesitation, then:

LISA: Yeah. Yeah, I should have chucked them out years ago.

TOM: That'd be great! His twenty-first is coming up—I'll pay you, of course. But are you sure?

LISA: Yeah. Yeah, I am. It's time. [*Shy*] Would you like to come to my place for lunch on Saturday? You can pick them up then.

TOM: I'd love to.

LISA: Cool. And you don't have to pay for them.

TOM: I don't know about that. I think I insist.

He yawns and puts his arm around her. LISA *yawns too.*

LISA: [*the yawn*] Oh… you've set me off.

She nestles into him, maybe drapes her leg across his.

Is this okay for your back?

TOM: It's fine. Your knees?

LISA: They're good…

She yawns again—at the exact same moment as TOM *leans in to kiss her. They laugh.*

Oh… that must have been like kissing a cave.

TOM: It was like pashing the entrance to Luna Park. What can I bring on Saturday?

LISA: Hmm… how about a nice bottle of wine?

TOM: Red? White?

LISA: Surprise me.

Lights fade…

We hear the first upbeat instrumental bars of 'Town Called Malice' from the album The Gift *by The Jam (1982) fade up through the darkness…the music sounds slightly scratched, as though it's being played on vinyl…*

◊ ◊ ◊

As the instrumental intro grows louder and louder the lights fade up and we're in a different space. This is Lisa's home.

Her living room is minimally suggested by a sofa and a desk with computer on top—but there's an adjoining bedroom that's a study in detail.

It contains a single bed, an old record player, haphazard piles of vinyl records, vintage New Musical Express *(*NME*) magazines, a chest of drawers crudely painted in a checked pattern, and piles of crumpled clothes—jumpers, shirts, shoes, jeans, bags, a black skinny tie—plus other forms of young male detritus.*

Early '80s concert posters for bands like The Sunnyboys, The Jam, The Clash, Simple Minds, Blondie and Stiff Little Fingers are plastered all over the walls. This room is stuck in a time warp from the early 1980s.

'Town Like Malice' is playing on the scratchy record player. A 20-year-old guy, DANIEL, *dressed in early '80s post-punk garb (short-sleeved button-down shirt, stove-pipe jeans, skinny tie—inspired by Paul Weller and early Elvis Costello), is fast asleep on the bed, still wearing his shoes. He's turned to the wall. A cigarette is smoking in an ashtray beside the bed.*

LISA enters, carrying a cardboard box. She nervously looks over at DANIEL *to make certain he's sleeping. Then she summons emotional strength and turns her back to him.*

The vocal kicks in. As Paul Weller rails about time being short and life being cruel, LISA *tiptoes to the record player and lifts the needle. The Jam falls silent.* LISA *puts the album back in its cover and puts the album into the box. Then she starts putting other albums into the box.*

Behind her, DANIEL *stirs. He wakes, looks over.*

DANIEL: Hey, what are you doing?

> *LISA stops guiltily.* DANIEL *is good-natured.*

[*Yawning*] Did you just turn off *The Jam*? That's sacrilege! I was listening to that.

LISA: You were passed out.

DANIEL: No, I was just giving my eyeballs a well-deserved rest.

> *He giggles.*

LISA: Are you stoned again?

DANIEL: I prefer the term shit-faced. [*He giggles again.*] What's with the box?

> *He gets up.* LISA *looks guilty.*

LISA: I was just… I saw this box and I thought that maybe I'd—

DANIEL: Will you stop trying to tidy my stuff? I told you, I've got a system—

LISA: What, chucking everything over your shoulder?

DANIEL: I just bought that album today, it's unreal. *The Gift*. You've got to hear it—

> *He retrieves the album from the box and takes the record out of its cover.*

Paul Weller was voted Most Wonderful Human Being by *NME* readers three years in a row—you can't keep him in a cardboard box.

> LISA *holds up the album cover.*

LISA: *This* is cardboard.

DANIEL: Yeah, but he's not sharing it with other bands who'd offend his musical sensibilities.

> *He takes out another album.*

What are The Doobie Brothers doing in here?

LISA: Oh, that one's mine.

> *She takes it.* DANIEL *throws his arm over her shoulder affectionately.*

DANIEL: You know, it's very sad that a woman of your intelligence has such shit taste in music.

LISA: Ew, you reek of nicotine and pot.

> DANIEL *giggles and gives her a squeeze.*

DANIEL: Where were you tonight?

> *She steps out of his arms.*

LISA: I told you. I was doing an interview for my new story—

DANIEL: The one about old people having babies?

LISA: You make them sound like geriatrics. They're middle-aged.

DANIEL: You said the fathers were fifty-something—

LISA: A couple of them. This guy tonight, my accountant Tom—he's umm, just fifty.

DANIEL: Just? That's halfway to a hundred! I reckon it's sick.

LISA: [*light*] You're so tolerant, aren't you?

DANIEL: You should've said no.

LISA: Why would I, Dan? Just because *I* don't want a baby… Older parents are a social phenomenon.

DANIEL: Isn't it *a?*

LISA: What?

DANIEL: It's social phenomen*a.*

LISA: No, that's plural. *Non* is singular. Social phenome*non.*

DANIEL: No, it's not.

LISA: Should we settle this with Google?

DANIEL: With what?

LISA: Never mind.

> *Her tone is light but she looks troubled.*

Why don't we just get rid of a couple?

DANIEL: Get rid of them? You mean chuck them out?!

LISA: It's time we had a good spring clean. Just the ones you don't listen to all the time—

DANIEL: I listen to all of them all the time! It's a well-known fact that it's impossible to have too many albums of the Post-Punk New Wave movement.

> *But* LISA *has just picked up the Sex Pistols'* Never Mind the Bollocks.

LISA: [*joking*] *Never Mind the Bollocks*, Dan, let's get rid of this—

> *She puts it in the box and* DANIEL *immediately removes it. This is repeated faster and faster—with each album, the tension escalates.*

DANIEL: [*removing it*] I'm not chucking the Sex Pistols—

LISA: [*putting one in*] Well, how many Clash albums do you actually need?

DANIEL: [*removing it*] All of them. Joe Strummer was 1981's Second Most Wonderful Human Being—

LISA: [*putting one in*] Okay, the Joy Division—

DANIEL: [*removing it*] No, that's their last album with Ian Curtis—

LISA: [*putting one in*] The Sunnyboys, then—

DANIEL: [*removing it*] They're not going anywhere.

LISA: There must be something you can spare? [*Picking up another one*] Bananarama—

DANIEL: [*snatching it back*] No, that stays with me—

LISA: Bananarama? You've got to be kidding.

In desperation, DANIEL *grabs an album and shoves it at her.*

DANIEL: Here. You can chuck this—

LISA: *Thriller*?

DANIEL: Courtesy of Aunty Lorraine, remember? I don't know when she bizarrely decided that I was a Michael Jackson fan. Take that and The Doobie Brothers.

LISA: No. While we're here and we're in the right frame of mind, we have to do this properly—

DANIEL: Do what? What frame of mind?

LISA: We have to bite the bullet, Dan—

She starts grabbing piles of albums and tossing them chaotically into the box. She's almost manic. DANIEL *watches, confused and horrified.*

DANIEL: Stop, stop! What are you doing? Put them back. *Stop!* [*Hurt, bewildered*] Why would you chuck my records away? What are you trying to do to me?

It's a metaphorical slap in the face that brings LISA *back to her senses.*

LISA: God, I'm sorry, Dan. I'm really sorry...

She starts taking the albums out of the box.

I don't know what I was thinking.

DANIEL: Me neither. You went all mental for a second.

LISA: Yeah. [*Holding up an album*] Mental as Anything.

DANIEL: [*with love*] Psycho.

He pulls her into a hug. She leans into him, breathing him in.

LISA: [*adoring*] You stink.

He starts tickling her. They both laugh as she wriggles and giggles.

Stop! Stop...!

DANIEL *picks up the* The Gift *album cover.*

DANIEL: So you've got to listen to *The Gift*, okay? Did I tell you what the first track's called?

LISA: What?

DANIEL: 'Happy Together'.

LISA: 'Happy Together'?

DANIEL: Yeah. It's our song, Lise.

> *He puts the needle down on the record and the musical intro starts. DANIEL starts jumping up and down like a pogo stick, legs and arms flying through the air, dancing with utter abandon.*

> *As the vocals kick in LISA watches, smiling. She can't help being infected by his joy.*

Come on, I dare you!

> *LISA laughs and starts jumping up and down with DANIEL. She hasn't perfected the pogo technique—far from it—but she's having just as much fun as him. While Paul Weller sings about being happy together until the end of time, they leap around the room laughing. But then—*

LISA: [*wincing*] Ohhh!

> *Pain shoots through her middle-aged knees. She stops dancing and bends in a hobble.*

My knees…

DANIEL: [*laughing*] Are you okay?

LISA: Chair…

> *As DANIEL helps her hobble to a chair, music and lights fade out…*

◊ ◊ ◊

A spotlight shines on LISA as she stands talking on the phone.

LISA: Oh, Tom. Hi it's me, Lisa Fitzgerald—oh, you probably didn't need the surname. I'm calling about those vinyl records—I'm sorry, but I don't think I'm ready to get rid of them after all. So, I guess there's no need for you to come over for lunch now. I'm sorry I didn't catch you in person—I'll, umm, put that Pilates receipt in the mail. Okay… bye.

> *She hangs up, feeling like an idiot.*

> *As the lights fade out, the sounds of young children's laughter fades up.*

◊ ◊ ◊

It's a new day. LISA *is sitting with her friend* JENNY, *forty-six, on a park bench.* JENNY *is peering anxiously into a pram, with a finger to her lip, urging* LISA*'s silence: Ssssh.*

As LISA *takes her digital recorder from her handbag,* JENNY *watches the baby and waits. After a few beats, she sighs with relief.*

JENNY: [*hushed*] Thank God. She's asleep.
LISA: Okay. Let's do—
JENNY: Ssssh!
LISA: [*lower*] Let's do this.

> *She presses the button on her digital recorder.*

Interview with Jennifer Bennett, forty-six-year-old mother of Ivy… four months?
JENNY: Five and a half. Already. Can you believe it? She's nearly onto solids.

> JENNY *smiles into the pram, but* LISA *stays focused on work.*

LISA: So. Jennifer—
JENNY: *Jennifer?*
LISA: We're here in an official capacity. *Jennifer. Ms Bennett.* It's quite a leap from corporate lawyer to stay-at-home mum.
JENNY: [*yawning*] Really? I hadn't noticed. How come I never see you anymore?
LISA: You're looking at me.
JENNY: Only in an 'official capacity'. You used to drop in all the time.
LISA: Just what you need with a new baby. Unannounced visitors.
JENNY: You're not unannounced visitors. Is it the vomit? The screaming? The poo? The chaos? What's so unappealing about our place lately?
LISA: Jen. Can we do this? What made you decide to have a baby at this stage in your life?
JENNY: Alcohol.

> *They laugh. Nearby a dog starts barking loudly.* JENNY *freaks.*

[*Low*] Shit! Bloody dog. [*Into the pram*] Please don't wake up… You've got no idea how hard she is to settle… I'm so sleep deprived. I found my keys in the fridge last night.
LISA: In the fridge?

JENNY: Ssssh!

LISA: [*lower*] Anyway. You were saying?

JENNY: What? What was I saying? Somebody shut that dog up. [*Yawning*] My brain's like a sieve.

LISA: I was asking you what made you decide to have a baby?

JENNY: Oh, yeah. I think biology crept up on me. I was like you—I never wanted kids.

LISA: I know. That's why I was asking.

The dog stops barking. JENNY *looks over, distracted.*

JENNY: Do you hear that? Silence. Thank God. Are they leaving?

LISA: Jen. Biology?

JENNY: Oh yeah, right. I didn't think I wanted kids, but when I turned forty, I started feeling this strange ache... It took me by surprise.

LISA: An actual ache?

JENNY: Yeah. When I saw a baby it would physically hurt, right here... [*She touches her chest.*] It was like this... yearning I'd never felt before. It was primal. I just had to have one of my own. And you know even when I look at her now, I still can't believe that she's mine.

LISA *feels unwelcome. Stirring, she quickly pushes away. The dog starts barking again.*

Shit.

Ivy starts crying.

Great. [*To the dog owner*] Thank you. Congratulations. [*To Ivy*] Ssssh, don't start... [*Shaking a rattle*] Look, here's the giraffe... Ssssh... Don't grizzle... Every time I think I'm going to get some peace...

LISA: You never told me about this ache before.

JENNY: You would have thought I was losing the plot—and you probably would've been right. Ssssh...

But Ivy cries louder. A frazzled JENNY *starts rocking the pram back and forth with one hand while shaking the rattle with the other. It's a difficult juggling act.*

LISA: So—you started trying to conceive when you were forty?

JENNY: Forty*ish.* Don't cry... It took a while for Nick to come around, but then we got on the shaggin' wagon.

LISA: Aggh. The mental picture.

JENNY: That's what conceiving a baby involves, in case nobody's told you.

Ivy's cries get louder.

Ivy, please. Ssssh. This is the worst thing—when they scream and you don't know why.

She hands LISA *the rattle.*

Can you shake this? What's wrong, darling? Have you got a sore tummy?

LISA *leans into the pram, shaking the rattle. Meanwhile* JENNY *rocks the pram with both hands.*

LISA: Look, Ivy, it's a fake giraffe without any limbs... See? Where are its legs? [*Back to* JENNY] How long did you try to conceive naturally?

JENNY: For about two years. I'm glad I built up some credits, because we haven't had sex for six months now. I can't believe I just told you that.

LISA: *Six* months?

JENNY: Yeah. I'm too exhausted. And poor Nick, I don't want him touching my boobs. She's sucking on them or I'm expressing with a pump. I feel like a dairy cow—it's *not* sexy. And no, you can't write that.

LISA: How's Nick coping with that?

JENNY: It's not ideal obviously, but he's nearly as stuffed as me. Honestly, I've got no idea how single mothers do it.

Ivy's cries grow louder.

Sssh... You can't be hungry already? Will Mumma get your bottle?

She stops rocking the pram and reaches underneath it for a large baby bag. Ivy's cries continue. LISA *stops shaking the rattle.*

LISA: So, you tried to conceive naturally until you were—forty-three? And then you started IVF?

JENNY: [*frazzled*] Don't stop.

LISA *resumes shaking the rattle. She watches as* JENNY *grabs the baby bag and starts taking out baby wipes, playsuits, cloth nappies, safety pins, baby food, tissues, etc.*

LISA: Have you got the kitchen sink in there too, Jen?

JENNY: Do you remember when I used to go out with just a lipstick and my purse? Now I feel like one of those packing mules. It takes forty minutes to get out of the house.

She takes out a bottle with milk in it and a container with formula. As she tips the formula into the bottle and shakes it vigorously, she throws a cloth over her shoulder to catch the baby's vomit.

LISA: [*shaking the rattle*] Look at the limbless giraffe, Ivy… Don't cry, your milk's coming… So? You started IVF?

JENNY: What?

She picks up Ivy out of her pram.

Here we go, darling… That's it… Mummy's got you… it's alright…

LISA watches as JENNY settles Ivy in her arms and puts the bottle into her mouth. Ivy stops crying. LISA finds herself transfixed. She keeps shaking the rattle.

Is that better, darling? Was that the problem?

The baby sucks.

[*Relieved*] She was hungry—she's got her father's appetite. You can stop now.

LISA stops shaking the rattle, embarrassed. She steers herself back on point, but the rattle is still in her hand.

LISA: So. How did it feel to embark on IVF at forty-three?

JENNY: It was terrifying… The process was so invasive, and my hormones were all over the shop. And the disappointment when it didn't work… it was horrible.

The baby suddenly farts loudly. They laugh.

Ivy! Manners.

LISA: Better out than in, eh? [*The smell*] Ew. I shouldn't have sat downwind.

JENNY: [*to Ivy*] We'll change you when you've finished feeding, okay? [*Yawning*] Third poo today. You cannot believe how much laundry I'm doing—I should just chain myself to the washing machine.

LISA laughs.

What's it like on the outside, Lise? I've almost forgotten. Tell me a story.

LISA: Hey, who's interviewing who?

JENNY: Come on. I'm covered in baby vomit. Humour me. How's work? Seen any good movies? Who's in government? I've forgotten. What are the young people wearing these days? And what are the grown-ups talking about?

LISA: Real estate, mainly. Nothing changes.

JENNY: And what about you? What's going on? Have you met anyone?

The tiniest hint of hesitation before:

LISA: Nope. Not lately. But hey, I'm sure I'll find a new bastard soon.

JENNY: Don't say that—even in jest. We're forty-five now—

LISA: Hhhmm, you're *forty-six*—

JENNY: Whatever. You've got to stop picking the wrong guys. It's not funny anymore.

LISA: It's kind of funny.

JENNY: It *used* to be funny—but, Lise, come on. You're so amazing. Why do you want to waste your time with—?

LISA: [*cutting across*] So I've had bad luck with blokes, so sue me. It's alright for you. There aren't too many Nicks out there.

JENNY: You're right. Thank God for Nick. I have to have sex with him. I must write that on a post-it note.

LISA *laughs. She finds herself looking down at Ivy.*

LISA: Your mummy's lost her tiny mind.

JENNY: I have. And it's all your fault, stinky girl…

LISA *watches as* JENNY *beams at her baby daughter, her eyes alight with joy. Her voice is soft and soaked with love.*

Are you Mummy's stinky little girl?

A wave of longing washes over LISA, *unbidden. It floors her. She leaps to her feet.*

LISA: You know what? I think I've got enough.

She tosses the rattle and her digital recorder into her handbag.

JENNY: What? But we've barely started.

LISA: I've got the gist—and I'm on a crazy deadline. [*Seeing the rattle in her handbag, flustered*] Oh, this is yours.

She hands it to JENNY.

Sorry to pinch your rattle, Ivy. [*Standing*] I've got to stop talking and start writing.

JENNY: *Now?*

LISA: Yeah. Time got away from me.

> *She pecks* JENNY's *cheek.*

Thanks for this. I'll call you, okay? Oh, and the photographer will be in touch too. [*A quick glance into the pram*] Bye bye, Ivy.

JENNY: Lise—

LISA: Bye. I'll call you.

> *As she walks off, we fade to black.*

◊ ◊ ◊

In the darkness the screen appears above the stage as Lisa's computer monitor. We see the words as she types them:

> 'Five and a half months into motherhood, corporate lawyer
> Jennifer Bennett, 46, admits to struggling with sleep deprivation—
> but there's a glow of joy in her tired eyes that's evident to her
> closest friends (full disclosure: I'm one of them).'

Lights up on the living room. LISA *is at her desk. She pauses, then types again:*

> 'But frankly, I've had it with her and her exhausted eyeballs, so how
> good a friend can I be?'

An extravagant yawn. DANIEL *is entering from his bedroom with a copy of* New Musical Express *(*NME*) and an unlit cigarette.*

LISA: At last he surfaces! Look what you're missing—it's gorgeous out there.

DANIEL: [*wincing*] Fuck, too much sunshine.

> LISA *watches fondly as he closes the curtains and plonks himself down on the sofa, lighting a cigarette.*

LISA: You're like a nocturnal exhibit at the zoo. I could charge admission to your room. [*David Attenborough voice:*] The Dan Fitzgerald rarely emerges during daylight, preferring to sleep deeply amidst his native habitat of cold pizza, pretentious English music magazines and empty beer bottles. But at night he emerges from his cave and performs his bizarre mating dance…

She pretends to jump up and down with her feet on the ground—it looks ridiculous.

… hoping to attract a female of his own species—

DANIEL: [*laughing*] What is that?

LISA: Just trying to spare my knees. I made some muesli—it's got cranberries and sunflower seeds. You want some?

DANIEL: No, thanks. You know I can't eat first thing in the afternoon.

He takes a drag on his cigarette instead.

LISA: What if I added some cancerous toxins? Would that tempt you?

DANIEL: Hilarious. Hey, did I tell you I've decided to write a gig review and send it in to *NME*?

LISA: Good on you!

DANIEL: Yeah, I'm going to write about The Sunnyboys at the Village Green last night. But I've got to decide on my signature style… Tortured young artist? Cynical muso? I don't want to sound like a fan.

LISA: God forbid.

DANIEL: But I don't want to sound like a wanker, either. [*Picks up the* NME] There's a Go-Betweens review in here somewhere—can you read it and tell me what you reckon?

He opens the NME *and starts flicking through it.* LISA *looks at the cover.*

LISA: *New Musical Express*, October 16, 1982. [*The cover*] Who's he?

DANIEL: Rat Scabies from The Damned.

LISA: Rat Scabies? This guy actually calls himself Rat Scabies? What's his brother's name—Faecal Matter?

DANIEL: [*laughing*] Rat founded The Damned with Captain Sensible. They've got that new album, *Strawberries*, you know the one where the lyrics sheet smells like strawberries? But I like 'Machine Gun Etiquette' better. It's not in here, must be in the Bananarama one. I think that's on the floor in my room somewhere…

DANIEL *yawns and starts heading back into his room.*

LISA: On your floor? Good luck… I heard a rumour there's carpet in there, but I've never actually seen it.

DANIEL *laughs and exits.*

The front doorbell rings. LISA *walks over to answer it.* TOM *is on the threshold, holding a bottle of wine.*

Tom?!

TOM: Lisa. Hi.

LISA glances back towards Daniel's bedroom and then stands on the spot with a forced smile. A couple of awkward beats pass.

Oh. Am I early?

LISA: No, I just wasn't... Oh, sorry, come in.

But she barely steps backwards. TOM *steps forward to kiss her lips, but* LISA *ducks sideways and he ends up kissing her somewhere near her ear.*

TOM: Sorry.

LISA: No, that's okay. Umm, didn't you get my message? I left a message on your mobile—

TOM: Oh. Gracie got her mitts on it—she's pressed all the buttons and reset everything. What was it?

LISA: I rang to say that I've decided to keep the records.

TOM: Oh. Okay. Sure. Your call.

LISA: I'm sorry. I should have thought before I offered—

TOM: No, that's okay. I don't blame you. It sounds like a bit of a treasure trove.

LISA: I hope your nephew won't be too disappointed?

TOM: Considering he didn't know about it, I think he'll cope okay.

He smiles. LISA *is reminded of just how much she likes him.*

LISA: Well, I hope I haven't wasted your time.

TOM: I'm here, aren't I? And the records were really just an excuse to spend some time with you without talking about your tax return— you have to give me that Pilates receipt, by the way.

LISA: You just talked about my tax return.

TOM: Yeah.

They smile.

LISA: Did Tony call you? The photographer? He wants to shoot you and Grace on Monday.

TOM: Yep, all organised. In a shock development, Grace wants to wear pink. Oh, and I brought you this. I couldn't decide between red and white, so I made a bold call—it's rosé.

> *As he steps forward to give her the wine,* LISA *subtly blocks his path again.*

LISA: Thanks, but I thought you weren't coming, so I haven't got lunch sorted. Sorry.

TOM: Oh. Okay…

> TOM*'s not sure whether this is a rejection.* LISA *glances back at Daniel's room.*

LISA: Could we do it another time?

TOM: Well, do you want to go out somewhere instead? I mean, now? My shout. If you'd like to?

> LISA *hesitates for a beat, then:*

LISA: You know what? I'd love to.

TOM: Great.

> *His mobile rings, he checks the screen.*

Sorry, it's Sue—I should get this. [*Answering*] Hi. What? Has she? No, I would've noticed. Alright—I'll take a look and call you straight back. [*Hanging up*] Sue thinks that Grace might have left her blankie in my car. I'll just be a minute—

LISA: I'll grab my bag and meet you out there.

TOM: Great.

> TOM *exits.* LISA *glances towards Daniel's room again and then stealthily tiptoes to her desk, picking up her handbag.* DANIEL *re-enters behind her.*

DANIEL: Did I just hear the doorbell?

LISA: What? Oh, yeah. It was my accountant.

DANIEL: On a Saturday?

LISA: Yeah, he's keen as mustard. [*Quickly qualifying*] I mean about work. Tax. He's umm, out at his car.

> DANIEL *immediately moves to the window.*

Don't stare out the window—

DANIEL: That old guy with the sensible family sedan?

LISA: He's not old—

DANIEL: [*laughing*] Fuck. His jeans are ironed.

LISA: They are not.

> *But she can't resist joining* DANIEL *at the window.*

DANIEL: They are. You could cut a sandwich with the crease in the middle, see? Fabulon Man. What did he want?

LISA: Actually, we're having lunch. So I'll see you later—

> *She's making a beeline for the front door, but* DANIEL *steps into her path.*

DANIEL: What?

LISA: We have to discuss my tax return.

DANIEL: But you said you'd read the gig review.

LISA: I will, but can't I do it later?

DANIEL: But I asked first! I need your professional opinion—I'm trying to nail down my style.

LISA: Well, why don't you try a few things while I'm out? I'm a freelancer, my tax is complex. There's a lot to discuss—

DANIEL: What? I can't believe what I'm hearing. Would you rather talk tax with that geriatric than help *me*? You don't actually *like* that boring old fart out there?

LISA: He's not a boring— [old fart]

> *But* DANIEL *is staring at her incredulously. She caves.*

No, of course I don't like him—not like that. You're right, you asked first.

DANIEL: Good on you, Lise. You're a star.

> *He gives her an affectionate kiss.*

> *The lighting state changes, and we hear the sound of a car door closing...*

◊ ◊ ◊

Outside, LISA *approaches* TOM. *He waves a little kid's blanket.*

TOM: It was under the passenger seat. I hate it when Sue's right—I know that's very mature of me. Do you mind if we take a detour—?

LISA: Tom. I'm really sorry, I've just remembered—I've got a doctor's appointment. It slipped my mind—I have to be there in half an hour.

TOM: Oh. Okay. I guess I should let you go, then. [*Is he being given the flick?*] Another time?

LISA: Umm, if I can—I've got a lot on. Can I call you and let you know?

> *He* is *being given the flick! And now he can't get out of there fast enough.*

TOM: Sure, no problem! Absolutely. Well, bye then. Just drop that Pilates receipt off sometime—

> *In his rush to get into his car, he drops the 'blankie'.* LISA *picks it up.*

LISA: Tom. The blankie…

TOM: Oh. Right. Yeah. Thanks.

> *As she hands it to him, their hands touch. It's almost more than* LISA *can bear.*

LISA: Bye…

> TOM *nods and exits.*

> *As* LISA *turns back for the house, the lights fade…*

◊ ◊ ◊

Fighting emotion, LISA *re-enters the living room.*

LISA: So show me this thing—

> *She stops, the room is empty.*

Dan? Dan?

> *She heads into Daniel's room. He's lying on his bed.* LISA*'s incredulous.*

What are you doing?

DANIEL: I'm a bit stuffed… thought I might go back to bed for a while.

LISA: You've got to be kidding! I just cancelled lunch.

DANIEL: So? You've been saved from a riveting chat about tax.

> *Annoyed,* LISA *grabs* DANIEL*'s pillow and hits him with it repeatedly.*

LISA: Sit up! You said you wanted to 'nail your style', so that's exactly what we're going to do.

> *She sits on his bed and picks up the* NME.

Show me this thing—

DANIEL: Here. The Go-Betweens did a gig in London, and I want to know if you like this guy's writing.

LISA: The Go-Betweens at the University of London, by David Dorrell…
[*Reading*] 'The Go-Betweens seem to sweat for your despair… their moaning Hades-bound sound was like a bum version of Echo's "Disease"… pity searching but wallowing in its own grave thoughts.' [*Laughing*] What? [*Reading more*] 'So dark that it was impossible to glean even a sinew of hope from the gloom-laden corpse… There was no soaring disquiet, no spirit-lifting heart-cry. The drums drove a tense but never tension-mounting set into the barbiturate coma…' [*Laughing*] This is pretentious crap.

DANIEL: You reckon?

LISA: Don't you?

DANIEL: Yeah, but I wanted to check. I'm planning to use less adjectives.

LISA: Good move. Keep it clean and simple, like The Sunnyboys' music. If you can reflect their light touch with your writing—

DANIEL: You don't have to tell me how to write it.

LISA: I thought you wanted me to help?

DANIEL: I wanted you to read the review. I can do the rest for myself.

LISA: But *will* you?

It's spontaneous, and it surprises them both.

DANIEL: What's that supposed to mean?

LISA: It means we've been here so many times before. You were going to interview *The Church*, remember? But when you couldn't get to them straight away, you just gave up—

DANIEL: [*pained*] Lise—

LISA: I worry about you, Dan. You left uni after one semester. You've had—what is it? Seven jobs in two years? And you've hated them all. But the Editor of *NME* isn't going to appear at the door and say, 'Is there anyone here who wants to be a music reviewer?' *You* have to make it happen.

DANIEL: [*defensively*] I know that—

LISA: It takes commitment.

DANIEL: Thanks for the tip.

LISA: I just want you to be happy. You're driving a courier van and you hate it.

DANIEL: So? We can't all be Little Miss Perfect with a cushy cadetship at *The Age* straight out of high school.

LISA: I worked my guts out for that cadetship—you know I arranged my own work experience in the holidays. You could do something like that too—

DANIEL: But I'm not you. When will everyone get that, instead of comparing us all the time? 'He's so hopeless, he's such a loser—why can't he be more like her?'

LISA: No-one's doing that.

DANIEL: Bullshit. And you know what really pisses me off? None of them will just admit that you're luckier than me.

> LISA *flinches. He's hit an extremely raw spot.*

LISA: Dan. Please don't say that I'm lucky.

DANIEL: You are.

LISA: But don't you get it? That makes me feel like I've taken luck from *you*...

> *Lights out...*
>
> *A clinical 'beep... beep...' fades up, in the darkness.*

◊ ◊ ◊

A slide appears: 'October 30, 1982'.

Lights up. We're now in an Emergency Department, simply suggested by eerie 'beeps'. LISA, *now 20, sits on a chair next to her mother* BARBARA, *clutching hands. They're both rigid with fear as they watch (imaginary) medical staff walk past—two sets of eyes following people travelling in different directions, like onlookers at a terrifying tennis match.*

BARBARA: Excuse me, nurse? I'm Barbara Fitzgerald and this is my daughter Lisa. We're waiting for news about—

LISA (20): Excuse me, can you tell us—?

> *They cut off as the nurse walks away. Silent tension. Someone passes in the opposite direction.*

Umm, excuse me, are you a doctor? No, wait—

BARBARA: Excuse me, a policeman told us to come here. He said Daniel Fitzgerald was brought here—

The person walks off in the other direction. Mother and daughter grip hands. Someone else appears, walking in the other direction.

LISA (20): Excuse me! Why won't you talk to us?

BARBARA: Please! We need to know—

LISA (20): Wait! Why won't anyone stop?

A DOCTOR *(real) approaches from the opposite direction. He looks sombre.*

DOCTOR: Mrs Fitzgerald?

BARBARA: Yes?

DOCTOR: I'm Dr McGrath. Could I have a word with you, please?

LISA *watches in terror as the* DOCTOR *leads* BARBARA *several feet away. He positions two chairs facing each other and seats* BARBARA *with her back to* LISA. *He speaks to her softly.* LISA *can't hear what he's saying, but she sees her mother put her head in her hands and her shoulders start heaving.* LISA *jumps up from her chair, yelling:*

LISA (20): No! No!

BARBARA: [*sobbing*] Sweetheart—

The DOCTOR *and* BARBARA *hurry over to her.*

LISA (20): No!

DOCTOR: I'm very sorry. Daniel died fifteen minutes ago—

LISA (20): No, you're a liar! You're a bloody liar!

BARBARA: He's not lying, sweetheart—

LISA (20): He *is!* He's lying—

She's pacing in manic circles. The DOCTOR *tries to touch her.*

DOCTOR: I'm sorry. I know this is a terrible shock—

LISA (20): Get off me! Why are you lying? Come on, they're lying, let's just go home.

BARBARA *manages to grab her arm, slowing her briefly.*

BARBARA: Sweetheart… sweetheart… [*To the* DOCTOR] I'm sorry…

DOCTOR: It's alright.

Tries to guide her to a chair.

Why don't you sit?

LISA (20): I said get off me!

She shoves him off and resumes pacing in manic circles.

DOCTOR: [*to* BARBARA] You're Catholic? I'll get the chaplain—
LISA (20): I don't want a chaplain, God can fuck off! I'm leaving—
BARBARA: Lisa, please—
LISA (20): Come on. It's all lies—

She tries to pull BARBARA *away but* BARBARA *grabs her and manages to still her. She wraps her arms around her heaving daughter.*

BARBARA: [*to the* DOCTOR] I'm sorry… she's his twin.

Long seconds pass as LISA *calms slowly into helplessness.*

DOCTOR: Would you like to see him?
LISA (20): [*frightened*] I can't…
BARBARA: You don't have to… you wait here.

But as the DOCTOR *and* BARBARA *step away:*

LISA (20): No, don't leave me! I'll come too…

The DOCTOR *leads them to the bed where* DANIEL *lies with his eyes closed. They're looking at him through glass.*

He looks like he's sleeping… maybe he is? [*Putting her palms up against the glass*] Dan… wake up… wake up…

But DANIEL *remains still and silent several beats, then* LISA *turns back to her mother.*

It's my fault. God gave me all the good luck.

As the lights fade slowly, we fade up the evocative chorus of 'The Bitterest Pill' by The Jam (1982)…

◊ ◊ ◊

As 'The Bitterest Pill' fades down into the darkness, a smiling photo of Jenny, Ivy and Jenny's husband Nick appears on the screen above the stage. Then another. And another.

Lights up. LISA *is flicking quickly through the shots on her laptop while* JENNY *looks over her shoulder. They're at Jenny's place—Ivy is sleeping in her pram nearby.*

LISA: He just sent me these. They look pretty good—

JENNY: [*yawning*] How can you tell when you're flicking so fast?

LISA: I can get the gist—

JENNY: I can't. Will you just—? Hey, stop.

> *She grabs* LISA's *hand, forcing her to stop clicking. Unfortunately it stops at a very unflattering shot of Jenny—her eyes are shut or she looks cross-eyed or whatever.*

LISA: [*teasing*] That's it—that's the shot I'm using.

> *Ivy makes a small grizzling sound from the pram.*

JENNY: Ivy! Don't even think about it…

> *She tip-toes to the pram. The baby falls quiet.* JENNY *turns back to* LISA, *hushed.*

Thanks for this. Nick only got the tickets today and both of the grandmas were busy—

LISA: You told me that already.

JENNY: Oh yeah. [*Yawning*] You're sure you'll be fine?

LISA: She sleeps, I write—

JENNY: Sssh!

LISA: [*lower*] She sleeps, I write. How hard can it be?

> JENNY *takes one more peek into the pram and then heads to the computer.*

Here. Let *me* take a look at these.

> *She takes the mouse and flicks through a few shots slowly.*

LISA: That one's nice.

JENNY: [*yawning*] Excuse me, how many chins? Oh, stuff it—I'm forty-six. That's how I look.

LISA: You look gorgeous, Jen. You're a yummy mummy.

JENNY: Not quite. I'm slightly past my 'best before' date.

LISA: Rubbish. You're a spunk.

JENNY: A spunk? Now there's a word I haven't heard in a while.

LISA: You're a big fat spunkrat. [*As* JENNY *laughs*] Dan said that once, remember?

JENNY: Dan did? Dan who? Oh shit, Lise, I'm sorry—

LISA: It's okay—

JENNY: I told you my brain was fried. Did Dan say that I was a spunk?

LISA: Yeah. Don't you remember? It was at roller skating that time in Year Seven. He said that if you weren't *my* friend, he'd think you were a bit of a spunk.

JENNY: I'd forgotten all about that... Mind you, Dan was twelve. Anything with a pulse.

◊ ◊ ◊

The lighting state changes. A slide appears above the stage: '1975'.

DANIEL *enters with a tea towel and gives* LISA *a dishwashing brush. They're now twelve years old and doing the dinner dishes.* BARBARA *hovers.*

BARBARA: [*embarrassed*] It's important for boys and girls to learn how to, umm, negotiate things with... the opposite sex. Did you find the film at school today helpful?

    LISA *and* DANIEL *laugh and squirm.*

It's not funny, sex is a normal part of life. Is there anything you'd like to ask? Dan, you could talk to Dad if you want to?

LISA (12) / DANIEL (12): [*simultaneously*] No, Mum! / No way!

BARBARA: Well, you know where we are.

    She practically runs out of the room. The kids wash and dry. DANIEL*'s drying style is slapdash, to say the least.*

LISA (12): You're not doing it properly.

DANIEL (12): Shut up, Lise. Have you had menstruation, yet?

LISA (12): No. Have you had a wet dream?

DANIEL (12): [*nodding*] Last week.

LISA (12): Really? What did it feel like?

DANIEL (12): Good.

LISA (12): Good? Like how?

DANIEL (12): Like... just *really* good.

LISA (12): And it wet your sheet?

    DANIEL *nods.*

Did you tell Mum?

DANIEL (12): Get out of it!

LISA (12): Well, what did you do with the sheet? Did you chuck it in the washing machine?

DANIEL (12): Why? It dried.

LISA (12): Oh, yuck!

DANIEL (12): Shut up! It happened the next day, anyway.

LISA (12): So that dried too?

DANIEL (12): It's kind of crusty.

LISA (12): Dan, you're revolting.

DANIEL (12): It's not as revolting as menstruation.

LISA (12): Yeah, that's disgusting... I wonder how come you've had wet dreams but I haven't menstruated?

DANIEL (12): I'm older than you.

LISA (12): By 15 minutes! Debbie Jenkins is menstruating.

DANIEL (12): Did she tell you?

LISA (12): No, she told Roseanne Bailey and Roseanne told Tania Perkins and Tania told Jenny and Jenny told me.

DANIEL (12): Does Jenny still like Graham Taylor? He's a bit of a poof.

LISA (12): He is not! *You're* a poof—

> *But* DANIEL *isn't listening anymore. He's distracted by the sound of 1970s NASA chatter coming from a television offstage.*

DANIEL (12): Hey, 'The Six Million Dollar Man's starting—

> *He drops his tea towel and exits.*

LISA (12): Dan, we haven't finished! Dan!

> *But he's gone.* BARBARA *re-enters.*

Mum. Dan just ran off and there's still wet dishes.

BARBARA: [*indulgent*] He's hopeless, isn't he?

> LISA *sighs. She bends down and picks up Daniel's tea towel. She starts drying.*

You're a good girl, Lise.

> *The lights fade...*

> *NASA chatter from 'The Six Million Dollar Man' opening credits bridge us into the next scene:*

VOICE-OVER: Steve Austin, astronaut. A man barely alive... Gentlemen, we can rebuild him. We have the technology...

◊ ◊ ◊

We're back in the present at Jenny's place. The tea towel is now a cloth nappy. LISA *is practising folding it.*

LISA: I feel like I've got too many triangles.

JENNY: We haven't talked about Dan in years…

LISA: [*the nappy*] Is this right?

JENNY: No, that triangle's supposed to be folded over the other triangles.

LISA: Why can't you use disposable nappies, like everyone else in the world?

JENNY: Because I'm a middle-class leftie who wants to make amends for the air-conditioning that I refuse to give up.

LISA: Fair enough.

    LISA *folds.* JENNY *watches her carefully.*

JENNY: Has Dan been on your mind lately?

LISA: Yeah. A bit. Things come along and remind me. I saw a doco on Kakadu the other night.

JENNY: A doco on Kakadu? But Dan was a punk.

LISA: But he wanted to be a park ranger first. Don't you remember?

    JENNY *shakes her head.* LISA *laughs.*

I think he was inspired by 'Skippy'. That lasted until we were about fourteen, but then The Sex Pistols came along. Do you remember when he sprayed 'DISCO SUCKS!' on the side of the bus?

JENNY: [*feeling bad*] Sorry.

LISA: Well, what do you remember about him?

JENNY: [*thinking*] I remember at the start of high school he was kind of nerdy, but then he got cooler and cooler… And I remember playing spin the bottle at your sixteenth party—

LISA: Spin the bottle! *I* forgot about that—

JENNY: And I had to pash him, and it felt really weird 'cause I knew him so well.

LISA: He always liked you. I think he would have asked you out, but you suffered by association with me.

    As the lights fade, an exuberant girlish squeal leads into the chorus of Bananarama's cover of 'Venus' (1982). As the gorgeous Keren, Sara and Siobhan sing about fire and desire…

◊ ◊ ◊

A slide appears: '1980'.

'Venus' fades down as the lights fade up...

LISA *is pounding on Daniel's bedroom door.* JENNY *is beside her. They both wear scrunchies in their hair.*

LISA (17): Dan, did you steal my highlighter pens again?

DANIEL (17): [*through the door*] Get lost!

LISA (17): We need them! We have to study. If you don't come out I'll tell Mum and Dad that you're smoking pot.

> DANIEL *emerges. He's stoned.*

DANIEL (17): [*grinning*] No you won't. [*Flirting*] Hi, Jenny.

JENNY (17): Hi, Dan.

LISA (17): It stinks in there. Quick, shut the door.

> DANIEL *shuts the door. He giggles.* LISA *and* JENNY *are half-disapproving, half-impressed.*

You're off your face. How can you study when you're so out of it?

DANIEL (17): I don't want to study. Just 'cause you love studying—

LISA (17): I don't, but it's HSC year. We have to do it.

DANIEL (17): [*to* JENNY] She's such a crawler.

LISA (17): Shut up, Dan. Mum and Dad won't let me go out unless I get everything done.

DANIEL (17): So? Just tell 'em you've done it.

LISA (17): But that's dumb! If I get bad marks I won't be able to be a journalist—

DANIEL (17): [*scoffing*] Yes you will. You're already sending all that stuff to magazines. You've got a letter from Ita Buttrothe!

LISA (17): Yeah, but she didn't put my thtory in, did she?

DANIEL (17): Little Miss Perfect.

LISA (17): Shut up, Dan—at least *I'm* trying. Mum and Dad are worried about you. If you don't work you won't get into uni—

DANIEL (17): [*to* JENNY] Don't you reckon she loves herself sick?

LISA (17): I do not. I'm just saying that it doesn't make sense not to study—

DANIEL (17): Shut up, you crawler.

LISA (17): You shut up, you pothead.

> DANIEL *giggles and now* LISA *starts laughing too.*

DANIEL (17): You think you're so good but you drink Blue Nun with your stupid friends. [*To* JENNY] What about when you brought her home in a taxi with spew all over her clothes?

> *But* JENNY *doesn't join in. She's starting to look perturbed.*

LISA (17): So? Alcohol isn't illegal.

DANIEL (17): It is if you're seventeen! And I know you've got a fake ID.

LISA (17): Everyone's got a fake ID! But I don't get drunk when I'm supposed to study, and neither does Jenny! Do you?

JENNY (17): [*sad*] Guys. This was such a long time ago.

LISA & DAN [17]: [*in unison*] What?

JENNY (17): Dan, how long is it since you died? Isn't it about twenty-five years?

> LISA *and* DANIEL *instinctively move closer together, locking* JENNY *out.*

DANIEL (17): So?

LISA (17): What's that got to do with anything?

> *Lights out.*

◊ ◊ ◊

Lights up. We're back in the present at Jenny's place. LISA *finishes folding the nappy.*

LISA: Victory! A folded nappy. But there are no guarantees I can do this again, so she's only allowed one poo.

> *She notices* JENNY *looking at her.*

What?

JENNY: Don't kill me, Lise, but… have you ever thought about therapy?

LISA: What?

JENNY: I've been thinking—maybe you should see someone? It might help you to find the right guy.

LISA: Who says I want to find the right guy? I'm having plenty of fun with the wrong ones.

> *But* JENNY *isn't laughing.*

Jen, it's okay.

JENNY: But do you honestly think that you'd even *know* the right guy if you met him?

LISA: Of course I would. I *did.*

JENNY: You *did?*

LISA: [*oops*] I *would.*

JENNY: You said you *did*—

LISA: I meant that I *would*—if it ever happened. Why are you on my back lately? It's not my fault that I've had bad luck.

JENNY: Are you sure about that—?

LISA: Won't you be late?

JENNY: [*looking at her watch*] Oh yeah. Shit. [*Grabbing her handbag*] You've got both our mobile numbers—there's milk in the fridge. You shouldn't hear a peep out of her, but if she grizzles, just rock the pram back and forth. [*Yawning*] We'll be home at 11—allegedly—but I'll be lucky to make it through the first act.

> *She gives Ivy a feather-soft kiss.*

Bye bye, darling… You be good for Aunty Lisa. [*To* LISA] You're sure you're okay?

LISA: Just get out of here so we can start the party.

JENNY: Alright, I'm going.

> JENNY *exits. Resisting an urge to peek at Ivy,* LISA *sits at her laptop and starts flicking through some of her typed notes.*
>
> *Ivy starts grizzling in her pram.* LISA *stops and waits, but the baby's grizzles intensify.*
>
> LISA *gets up and walks to the pram. She rocks it gently back and forth…*

LISA: Ivy, you're supposed to be asleep… Sssh, it's okay… [*She grabs the giraffe rattle and shakes it.*] Look, it's Mr Giraffe… or is it Ms? It's hard to tell without genitalia…

> *But the baby starts crying.*

Oh, sweetheart, what's wrong?

> LISA *lifts Ivy out of the pram. She rocks the baby in her arms.*

Ssshhh… It's okay, I'm here…

> *Ivy stops crying.*

That's better, isn't it? Yes, it's Aunty Lisa…

LISA *drinks in Ivy's smell. Suddenly there's only her and this tiny child and the scary new yearning that tugs at the core of her. Confronted, she tries to snap herself out of it.*

Let's choose a pic and get this over with, eh? [*She starts flicking through the photos.*] What do you think, Ivy? This one? That's a good angle for you... but this one shows off your complexion... [*etc*]

After several shots of Jenny, Nick and Ivy, the photos change to Tom and his little daughter Grace, also snapped for Lisa's story. They're cuddling, kissing, clowning around; Grace's chubby little arms wrapped around Tom's neck.

LISA *falls silent. As she stares at the screen, the lighting changes to a fantasy state... and now suddenly Lisa is in the photos too: holding Grace in her lap, laughing and hugging Tom, being kissed on both cheeks by father and daughter...*

LISA *shakes her head as though to clear it.*

[*Joking*] Woh. Your Aunty Lisa needs to get out more.

She clicks on the mouse. The screen goes black.

I really have to write.

She puts Ivy back in her pram, but the baby starts grizzling. She picks her up again.

Ssssh, it's okay. Okay, come back then... Is that better, Ivy?

The baby stops crying.

It is? Good...

She stands with the baby snuggled in her arms, rocking her from side to side.

Lights fade...

◊ ◊ ◊

Lights up. LISA *and* TOM *are in a cafe. They have drinks in front of them, and their menus are sitting on the table.*

TOM: [*smiling*] I wasn't expecting you to ring. I thought you'd given me the flick.

LISA: No. I'm sorry about the other day, things fly out of my mind sometimes. Speaking of which—while I remember… [*Reaching into her handbag, she pulls out a receipt.*] I brought my Pilates receipt.

TOM: The missing piece in the tax return puzzle. Thanks.

LISA: Are you still thinking about Pilates?

TOM: I probably should be.

LISA: How's your back?

TOM: It's not bad, but I wasn't expecting a hardcover menu—I might need your help to lift it.

LISA: I'm not sure that my knees could absorb the load.

> *They laugh.*

TOM: What have you been up to, today?

LISA: You first.

TOM: Me? Nothing exciting. I did the grocery shopping and mowed the backyard, and on the way here I stopped at the cemetery. [*As* LISA *reacts*] You asked. Mum used to visit Dad twice a week, but she's got Parkinson's now and she's not too mobile. She worries about him… so I take him flowers most weekends, try and keep him nice.

> LISA *finds herself gazing at him: he's so gorgeous.*

Your turn.

LISA: Well… I swam some laps first thing, and then I went to Victoria Market. I love all the colour and the smells and sounds—it makes the whole morning disappear.

TOM: I should have tried that—my morning dragged. [*Shy*] I was looking forward to seeing you.

LISA: [*shy*] Me too.

TOM: So we're on the same page? This isn't just about Pilates receipts and tax returns? It's more than that?

LISA: Of course it is. *I* don't want to talk about tax.

TOM: That's just what I wanted to hear.

LISA: You're very honest, aren't you?

TOM: Am I?

LISA: Most people try and hide their feelings.

TOM: I'm too lazy for that.

> LISA *laughs.*

I guess I just don't see any point in keeping secrets.

Speaking of which, DANIEL *suddenly strolls up to the table.*

DANIEL: [*cheeky*] Lise! Wouldn't Meals on Wheels have been simpler?

   LISA*'s horrified look: What are you doing here?*

Just passing, saw his walking frame out the front.

   Grinning, he sits down between them.

TOM: I guess we should think about ordering.

   TOM *puts on his glasses.*

DANIEL: That's it, granddad, put on your bifocals. [*Calling to an unseen waiter*] Somebody get this old bloke a bib!

   As TOM *reads the menu,* LISA *mouths at* DANIEL.

LISA: [*silent*] What are you doing here?

DANIEL: I knew you'd be bored shitless. Look at this geriatric. I hope he's going to order the soup so he doesn't damage his dentures.

TOM: [*the menu*] Lisa, what do you think?

   LISA *tries valiantly to ignore* DANIEL.

LISA: [*the menu*] Umm, I like the look of the sausage.

DANIEL: [*looking at* TOM*'s crotch*] You wouldn't like the look of *his*. I'm telling you, Lise, limp and shrivelled. And I bet his balls are all old and saggy. [*Lifting the tablecloth to look*] Yep, you can see them— they're right next to his knees.

TOM: I think I'll have the meatballs.

   DANIEL *laughs loudly and nudges* LISA, *who's trying hard not to look at him.* TOM *puts his menu down and smiles across at her.*

I'm glad we've finally made this happen.

DANIEL: Made what happen? [*With a hint of genuine sympathy*] The poor old bastard thinks this is a date—you'd better set him straight.

LISA: I'm glad too.

DANIEL: [*surprised*] Lise.

TOM: You look great.

LISA: Thanks. So do you.

DANIEL: What are you doing? Don't lead the sad old accountant on.

TOM: How about a glass of wine? Will I see what they've got?

   TOM *picks up the wine list.* LISA *still tries to ignore* DANIEL, *but he moves his face up close to hers so she can't avoid his eyes.*

DANIEL: I know you want to be nice, but he thinks you *like him*—it's kind of pathetic. Don't let him make a dick of himself.

> DANIEL*'s pull is too powerful*—LISA *caves.*

LISA: [*to* TOM] Umm, will you be able to deduct all my Pilates sessions, or only a percentage?

TOM: Pardon? Oh, I should be able to claim up to seventy per cent… The photo shoot seemed to go well.

LISA: I know. I've seen the pics—Grace looks just like you! She's got the same colouring, and your curly hair—

DANIEL: [*warning*] Lise.

LISA: So, it's still appropriate to average my income?

TOM: What? Ah, yeah… you still have good years and leaner years, so I think that remains appropriate. If you went into full-time employment, we'd obviously have to reassess—

DANIEL: This old bloke talks like he's reading the phone book.

TOM: But seeing you've been freelance for such a long time, and you don't envisage that changing—

DANIEL: [*with a mock yawn*] Trying to… stay awake…

TOM: —I think we should stick with the averaging, at least for the foreseeable future.

> DANIEL *drops his head on the table and starts snoring loudly.* LISA *tries to push him away with her elbow.*

How's your story going?

> DANIEL*'s snores increase in volume.* LISA *pushes harder with her elbow.*

LISA: Pardon?

TOM: Are you okay?

LISA: Itchy elbow… it's fine.

> *She stops trying to push* DANIEL *away and rests her arm on the table.*

TOM: Your story. How's it going?

> *He shyly reaches over and takes her hand.*

DANIEL: Hey, she doesn't want to hold your clammy old paw. [*To* LISA] He's emptied his colostomy bag with that hand.

But LISA *wraps her fingers around* TOM*'s.* DANIEL *is surprised and little alarmed.*

Lise. What are you doing?

LISA: My story? It's slower than I'd like. I've had writer's block, which is rare for me, but I'll get there—

As LISA *is speaking,* DANIEL *starts whispering into her ear.*

DANIEL: Saggy old balls… saggy old balls… saggy old balls… [*Then suddenly anxious*] You don't actually want to touch his saggy old balls?

LISA *abruptly withdraws her hand.*

LISA: Umm, I was wondering whether I should stop paying my GST quarterly? I thought maybe if I paid annually instead, I could put my tax money aside and into some kind of term deposit?

TOM *feels slapped.*

TOM: Lisa. You told me you didn't want to talk about tax.

DANIEL: Why the fuck did you tell him that?

TOM: Is this about work, or about you and me?

LISA *hesitates.* DANIEL*'s alarm is growing.*

DANIEL: *You and him?!* In his dreams! Tell him he's dreaming. [*Panicking*] Lise, tell him.

TOM: Lisa?

They're both waiting. LISA *glances to* DANIEL. *There's very real fear in his eyes.*

DANIEL: What are you waiting for? Fuck, just say it!

LISA *can't bear to see* DANIEL *so frightened. He wins—again.*

LISA: [*to* TOM] The truth is, I *did* come to talk about tax—but that doesn't mean we can't have a nice… client-to-accountant chat.

TOM: You know what? I misunderstood, and I don't think that's entirely my fault… But anyway… The fact is, I've had all the rejection I can take for one year, and I like you too much to expose myself to more—

DANIEL: Spare us the details, old man.

TOM: *I* didn't come here to talk about tax, and we both know that.

LISA: Well. Okay. Can we go to your office to talk about tax?

DANIEL: Great idea! I'll come too.

TOM: Actually, I think it's probably best if you find another accountant.

LISA: What? Why?

TOM: I think that'll be the best thing for everyone. [*Pulling out her receipt*] Here's your Pilates receipt—I'll send you the rest of your file in the mail.

LISA: Really? But are you sure that's necessary? You've always done such a great job.

TOM: I know a lot of other good people. I'll send you some recommendations... There doesn't seem much point in ordering, does there? Why don't I just get the bill?

DANIEL: [*victorious*] Yeah, you do that, granddad.

> *As* TOM *heads off* DANIEL *plonks himself down in Tom's seat. He's jubilant—but* LISA's *bereft.*

> *Lights fade...*

◊ ◊ ◊

In the darkness, the screen above the stage is Lisa's computer monitor again. We see the words as she types them:
> *'Carlton accountant Tom Flannery, 50, is the adoring dad of three-year-old Grace.'*

Lights up. LISA *is sitting at her desk, struggling with the confronting story. She pauses for a beat, then quickly types:*
> *'It's just a shame a disk has slipped in his withered old back, so he can barely pick the poor kid up.'*

But it's not funny, it's just depressing.

LISA: Shit.

> *She puts her head in her hands. Meanwhile in Daniel's room, Sid Vicious starts warbling his discordant cover of 'My Way' at maximum decibels.*

[*Annoyed*] Dan! I'm trying to write!

> *Sid continues.* LISA *gets up and marches into Daniel's room.*

Will you turn that—

> *She trips on a knapsack that's lying on the floor.*

Shit! What's that doing there?

She picks it up and throws it at DANIEL. *He immediately opens it to look inside.* LISA *heads for the record player.*

I can't hear myself think over bloody Sid Vicious—

DANIEL: [*looking in the knapsack*] Have you seen my black skinny tie?

LISA: [*can't hear him*] Your what?

She lifts the needle. Sid falls silent.

Thank God.

DANIEL: [*throwing the knapsack down*] Have you seen my skinny tie?

LISA *picks up the* Sid Sings *album cover.*

LISA: Look at him—he looks as hideous as he sounds.

DANIEL: [*teasing*] You're hot for him.

LISA *shudders as she puts the record back in its cover. Meanwhile* DANIEL *keeps looking for his tie amidst his piles of albums, bags, shoes, clothes, loose papers,* NME *magazines, etc.*

Do you know how Sid got his name?

LISA: No-one else wanted it?

DANIEL: Johnny Rotten's pet ferret bit him.

LISA: His pet what?

DANIEL: Johnny Rotten had a pet ferret called Sid, and it bit John Ritchie—that was Sid before he was Sid. And John Ritchie said, 'Sid's vicious', so Johnny Rotten decided to call John Sid Vicious.

LISA: It's a shame the ferret didn't bite his head off and spare us all from this excrement.

DANIEL: [*amused*] He couldn't play bass for shit, could he? *Or* sing.

LISA: So why do you listen?

DANIEL: Because I want to. Sid's not *normal*—he's sticking it up all the mindless middle-class sheep.

LISA: The mindless, middle-class sheep like me?

DANIEL: No, not you. The mindless, middle-class sheep like the old guy with the saggy old balls.

LISA: Can we please not talk about Tom? I'm never going to see him again—you've made sure of that. So why can't you just be gracious in victory and forget the guy even exists? As soon as I've finished this bloody story, that's what *I* intend to do.

DANIEL: Okay, okay. Don't have a fit.

LISA: I'm not. Look at this mess. No wonder you can't find your tie.

DANIEL: Will you help me look? I need it tonight—

> As LISA *starts looking through piles of clothes and records and books and* NME *magazines and shoes, etc,* DANIEL *picks up Blondie's self-titled LP from 1976.*

I'm going out with a girl who looks like her.

LISA: You're going out with an actual girl who looks like Debbie Harry when Debbie Harry looked like that?

DANIEL: Yeah.

LISA: How very unfortunate for her.

DANIEL: [*laughing*] She's got blonde hair that's black at the back and big blue eyes—she wears black eyeliner and it looks really cool. And bright red lipstick.

LISA: That's great. Does she have anything else going for her? A name? A job? A personality?

DANIEL: Her name's Helen. She's a psych nurse. I met her at North's.

LISA: So she's a punk, like you?

DANIEL: I'm not a punk.

LISA: Yeah, okay. Punk/Mod/Urban/New Wave, whatever you call yourself.

DANIEL: I don't call myself anything. You're the one who feels like you have to call me something.

LISA: As long as I don't call you late for dinner, eh?

DANIEL: [*in an old lady voice*] That's very funny, love.

LISA: You know, you don't just sound like Aunty Lorraine, you're starting to look like her too. [*Peering into a chest of drawers*] Oh, found your tie—

DANIEL: Unreal. Where was it?

LISA: Right at the back, stuck between two drawers—

> *She pulls it out and gives it to him.*

DANIEL: Thanks, Lise—

LISA: This top drawer's full of so much crap. No wonder you can't— [*Gingerly pulling something else out*] Oh yuck! What's a dirty hankie doing in there?

DANIEL: That's got Steve Kilby's autograph on it. The Church.

LISA: I know who Steve Kilby is. You gave him a *dirty* hankie?

DANIEL: No, I blew my nose after he signed it.

LISA: What was the point of that? You'll have to wash it now.

DANIEL: [*cheeky*] No, I won't.

He grabs the hankie and puts it back in the drawer.

LISA: You think that's appealing on some bizarre level? It's just revolting.

DANIEL *just laughs.*

You're such a [*searching for the words*] … twenty-year-old.

DANIEL: Oh, derr.

But LISA*'s not smiling. As she looks at* DANIEL*, she finds herself suddenly filled with a new sense of weariness—and resignation. She starts leaving the room.*

Lise. Where are you going?

LISA: I don't think I'm up for this right now.

DANIEL: Up for what?

LISA: *You*, Dan. Your stories, your stuff… I'm just… I'm getting tired of it.

DANIEL: Lise, wait. I'm sorry. Do I talk about *my* shit all the time?

LISA: We both do.

DANIEL: I didn't realise. Why didn't you say?

LISA: I didn't realise either.

DANIEL: Well, don't go. Come and sit down. Please? We'll talk about whatever *you* want. Come on, Lise. I mean it.

LISA *acquiesces. She sits down on his bed.*

What do you want to talk about?

LISA: I don't know… Films or cooking? Politics, maybe?

DANIEL: Fuck, I could talk politics all day! Isn't Maggie Thatcher a bitch?

LISA: Maggie Thatcher…

DANIEL: Yeah. She was voted 1982 Creep of the Year by *NME* readers— two spots above Ronald Rea*gun*.

LISA: Two spots? Who came second?

DANIEL: Sting did.

LISA: Sting?

DANIEL: Yeah, he's a wanker. But Thatcher and Rea*gun* are fucking fascists. They don't give a shit about all the poor workers they're forcing onto the dole queues. And what about Brixton? Unemployment in blacks is fifty-five per cent—no wonder they're so pissed off they riot. But Thatcher's such a racist she doesn't care, she just says they're crims. And she won't spend money on the inner cities because 'you can't buy racial harmony'—

LISA: [*exploding*] Dan, it's 2007!

DANIEL: [*stung*] I know that.

LISA: Yeah, you know it in theory, but you don't have a clue how much the world's changed—

She picks up the Thriller *album and waves it at him.*

Michael Jackson is white.

DANIEL: What?

LISA: He's white with a tiny pointy nose. And Princess Di's been dead for ten years. And Sonny and Cher's cute little girl—you know Chastity? She's a bloke.

DANIEL: [*bewildered*] What?

LISA: There's this thing called DNA—they could take that old snot off your hankie and identify you out of a billion people. And a machine called the Rover's been to Mars and sent back photos all by itself. And people can talk to each other on their computers from anywhere in the world for free and see each other at the same time. And we've all got mobile phones we keep in our pockets 'cause they're smaller than your cigarette packs—and you type in a message and press a button and beep! It appears on another phone. And emails have superseded faxes and the word 'Google' is in the dictionary.

DANIEL: Goodle? What does it mean?

LISA: It's a search engine on the World Wide Web—don't even get me started on *that*. And you know what else? No-one buys albums anymore. There's an online shop called iTunes where you can buy individual songs, and you download those onto your iPod—

DANIEL: Your what?

LISA: [*over him*] And it's digital so the music can't get wrecked like when you spilled beer on 'London Calling'— [*Which reminds her...*] Oh, and Joe Strummer's dead.

DANIEL: Joe Strummer died?!

LISA: Five years ago. And Paul Weller just had a hip replacement. Actually, I made up the hip replacement—I'm just trying to illustrate my point. It's 2007, everything's changed—Oh, except Sting is still a wanker.

She stops, she's exhausted herself. DANIEL *is helpless and silent— his confidence has been knocked right out of him.* LISA *can't help feeling mean. A long silence, then:*

I'm sorry… that was mean.

Silence. She watches him anxiously.

Dan? Say something.

DANIEL: I don't know what to say… I should have realised this sucks for you.

LISA: It doesn't suck.

DANIEL: [*sincerely*] Yes, it does. I'm sorry, Lise. Am I stuffing your life up?

LISA: [*yes*] No! Of course not.

DANIEL: I don't want to stuff up your life. How can I change things? What can I do?

LISA: You can't do anything, isn't that the whole point?

She hugs him.

It's okay… Now I've got all that off my chest, I won't need to talk about it again.

DANIEL: Really?

LISA: [*nodding*] Yeah. I was just venting.

DANIEL *looks hugely relieved.*

DANIEL: So what do you want to talk about now?

LISA: Let's not talk about anything.

DANIEL: Now you're talking.

He grins and lies back down, turning his face to the wall. LISA *remains sitting on the edge of his bed. She stares into space with a sense of deep sadness.*

Lights slowly fade…

◊ ◊ ◊

As the lights fade up, JENNY *is entering with cardboard boxes. She looks around the room, surprised and saddened by what she sees.*

JENNY: Oh, Lise… Why didn't you tell me you'd kept his stuff?

LISA: I don't know… I've told you now. [*Taking a box*] We've got to get rid of it all, okay?

JENNY: Absolutely. I can sell it on eBay. Or we can chuck it. Or give it away. Whatever you want.

LISA: I just want it gone before I change my mind.

JENNY: Okay, let's do it. Will I start with his clothes?

LISA: [*nodding*] I'll pack his records.

> LISA *starts putting Daniel's albums into a box while* JENNY *picks up clothes and throws those in another, oblivious to* DANIEL *sleeping on the bed behind her.*

> *After a few beats* LISA *looks up and sees* JENNY *pick up Daniel's black skinny tie. Behind her,* DANIEL *stirs restlessly in his sleep.* LISA *panics.*

Ah no, not that.

> *She takes it and slings it around her neck.*

This was his favourite tie—

JENNY: I thought you wanted to get rid of it all?

LISA: This is skinny, it doesn't take up any space. [*Reacting to* JENNY's *worried look*] I'm only keeping this, I promise.

JENNY: Are you sure?

> LISA *nods.*

Okay… Well, maybe we'll work up to his clothes.

> LISA *resumes putting records in the box.* JENNY *turns her attention to Daniel's* NME *magazines and music posters. She throws the* NMEs *into a box and then reaches up to pull a Sunnyboys poster off the wall.* LISA *looks up and sees her.*

> *Behind her,* DANIEL *rolls over to face them. He's still asleep but he's tossing and turning—it seems he could wake at any moment.*

LISA: No, leave that there! The Sunnyboys were his last-ever gig. And it's so nice and bright—it's a good piece of artwork for the wall. People pay a fortune for retro posters.

JENNY: But is that why you want to keep it?

LISA: Jenny. It's my stuff, okay?

JENNY: I thought it was *Dan's* stuff and that's the whole point? I'm sorry. Okay, if you say so. We'll leave it.

> LISA *nods. Behind* JENNY, DANIEL *seems to settle back into sleep.* LISA *sits down on the bed in front of him, just in case, and reaches for records on the floor underneath. Meanwhile* JENNY *looks around, not sure what to try and pack up next. She opens the drawer. After a couple of beats she pulls out the used hankie.*

A twenty-five-year-old snotty hankie. I'm sure we can get rid of this—

> *Behind* LISA, DANIEL *stretches and murmurs.*

LISA: No. That's got Steve Kilby's autograph on it. The Church.
JENNY: I know who Steve Kilby is.
LISA: And nobody wants a used hankie.
JENNY: I was thinking we'd throw it away.
LISA: No!

> *She grabs the hankie and clutches it to her chest.*

JENNY: Lise. Do you want me here or not?
LISA: I don't know…

> *As* JENNY *waits,* DANIEL *tosses and turns and pushes against* LISA.

No, I don't. I'm sorry.

> DANIEL *relaxes back into sleep.*

JENNY: Okay, let's stop, but why don't I stay for a while? You might change your— [mind]
LISA: No, I think you should go. [*Reacting to* JENNY's *worried look*] I'm fine, Jen—you get back to Ivy. I just… I guess I'm not quite ready for this. [*As* JENNY *still hesitates*] I'm fine. We'll just do it another time.
JENNY: [*reluctantly*] Okay. But I'm leaving the boxes, and I want you to call me as soon as you're ready. It doesn't matter what time, what day—I'll work something out with Ivy. Just call me, okay?
LISA: Okay.

> *She hugs her.*

Thanks so much for coming, Jen.

> *They exit Daniel's room and head for the front door.*

I'm sorry for wasting your time.

JENNY: It's not *my* time you're wasting. It's all falling into place for me, Lise. I'm sure this must why you're so stuck.

LISA: [*confronted*] Stuck?

JENNY: You know you're stuck.

LISA: Bye, Jen.

> JENNY *exits.* LISA *is left alone to contemplate her words, with Daniel's tie slung around her neck and his snotty hankie clutched tight in her hand.*

I'm not stuck…

> *Lights fade…*

◊ ◊ ◊

Lights up. TOM *is at his desk in his office.*

TOM: [*into the phone*] Sue, it's only a cold—day care said she's doing fine… Yes, she's got her blankie… What? Why would we need to swap nights? Of course I've got kids' Panadol, I'm not a complete idiot.

> *He glances up as* LISA *appears in his doorway, holding a box of records.* TOM *is thrown.*

I have to go, I'll call you tonight. Bye. [*Cool*] Lisa, hi.

LISA: Can I come in?

> *He gestures: Sure. She enters, clearly nervous. She holds out the box.*

I've re-thought my re-thinking. I want you to have these records after all.

TOM: No thanks.

LISA: Oh. Are you sure? I've got Banarama in here! They're going for free.

TOM: Thanks anyway, but I've already sorted my nephew's birthday.

LISA: Oh. What did you get him? Can I take a seat?

TOM: I've got a client arriving in a few minutes.

LISA: I'll be quick. I came to give you this, too—

> *She reaches into her handbag and pulls out a business card, handing it to him.*

My Pilates teacher Ingrid—she's fantastic, my knees are in love with her. I've checked and you could get a discount because I introduced you.

TOM: [*bemused*] Thank you.

LISA: Actually, there's a vacancy in my studio session—six o'clock on Tuesdays.

TOM: [*what the hell?*] I should get ready for this meeting—

LISA: How's Grace? I heard your call. Has she got the flu?

TOM: It's just a cold. She'll be fine.

LISA: And Colonel Klink?

TOM: He's fine too. Last seen licking his genitals.

> LISA *laughs a bit too loudly.*

I have to prepare for this client—

LISA: Could we have lunch afterwards?

TOM: I thought we decided not to have lunch?

LISA: Let's un-decide. Maybe we could keep in touch and make it a regular thing?

TOM: Why would we do that?

LISA: As friends… former colleagues… whatever. We've known each other for ten years—it seems a shame to just write that off. The odd lunch or coffee couldn't hurt, could it?

TOM: Lisa. Why the hell are you here?

LISA: I like you.

> *It's clearly heartfelt.*

TOM: Then have dinner with me.

LISA: I can't, I'm sorry. I can only have lunch. I know that sounds weird, but… couldn't we just keep in touch?

TOM: Sorry, that doesn't work for *me*. Now if you don't mind, I've got things to do—

LISA: Of course. I shouldn't have come…

> *She picks up the box of records, but before she can even get to her feet* TOM*'s compassion gets the better of him.*

TOM: Lisa, wait… What the hell is this all about?

LISA: I just… My life's complicated.

TOM: Okay. How?

LISA: I'm sorry. I can't explain it—but please believe me.

TOM: Believe what? My life's complicated too—my wife left me for my best mate and took my daughter with her. So you'll have to forgive me if I'm not in the mood to be messed around.

LISA: The last thing I want is to mess you around—

TOM: Really? Then what do you call all of this? 'Come over to my place—no, go away. I've changed my mind again, let's have lunch. I'm here because I'm interested in you—well, actually, I'm only interested in tax. But on third thought, I really do like you, but I'll only see you for lunch now and then. I'd like to be more than friends but lunch will have to be good enough and I won't tell you why—you'll just have to believe me.' What is this, high school? Give me something I can understand.

LISA: I really want to explain, but…

> *She trails off.*

TOM: But you're not going to?

LISA: I can't. It's umm… a loyalty issue.

TOM: [*misinterpreting*] A loyalty issue?

LISA: I'm sorry. I wish I could tell you why.

TOM: You know what? Why is irrelevant. Something—or *someone*—is more important and that's all I need to know. I'd like you to leave now.

LISA: No! I didn't mean that, not like you think—

TOM: You don't mean a lot of things.

LISA: Tom, please—

TOM: Save it. I've had enough emotional abuse for one year.

LISA: I'm so sorry I can't explain all this properly. If it was just up to me—

TOM: Oh, give me a break—it *is* up to you. I don't know who else is in your life and frankly I don't care right now—but at least be real. This is all about *you* and how *you* want to construct your life and who you choose to stuff around while you do it. So why don't you take some responsibility?

LISA: I'm sorry—

TOM: I don't want to hear it. Just grow up.

> *Conversation over.*

◊ ◊ ◊

LISA *arrives home and slams down the box of records.* DANIEL *emerges from his room. He smiles at her affectionately.*

DANIEL: Here she is. Why aren't you chained to your desk?

> *He's expecting a hug, but instead she slaps him hard across the face.*

LISA: How could you be such a fucking fool?!

> DANIEL *lurches backwards, stunned.*

How could you be so bloody stupid?

DANIEL: Lise? What's—?

LISA: You're a fucking moron!

> *She goes to slap him again but he grabs her hand in time.*

DANIEL: Fuck. Lise! What are you doing—?

LISA: Who gives their girlfriend their only motorbike helmet? Catch a bus. Get a lift. Get a taxi. What kind of idiot are you? You didn't even know her that well—why would you throw your life away for someone you've known for a couple of months?

DANIEL: Shit. Lise—

LISA: Why, Dan?

DANIEL: I didn't know I was throwing my life away.

LISA: Well, guess what? You're dead! [*She throws herself down into a chair.*] It's not fair. Why am *I* acting like such a fool when you're the one who was so bloody stupid? I'm hurting people who don't deserve it and I've stuffed a great story because I can't write it. *I'm* supposed to be the successful one, but I'm messing everything up… I suppose you think it's about time?

DANIEL: No, of course not. I'm proud you've got your shit together.

LISA: I used to. Now my shit's all over the place.

DANIEL: Lise…

> *He tries to hug her but she resists.*

LISA: But it's such a waste. We could have had families. We could have had barbecues with our kids, they could have grown up together. Your wife could have been my bridesmaid and you could have been best mates with my husband—we could have grown old together, but instead we're both acting like twenty-year-olds.

DANIEL: *You're* not.

LISA: I am. I'm behaving like a peri-menopausal teenager, and it's all because of your bloody helmet.

DANIEL: I'm sorry, Lise. I'm really sorry. I was just trying to do the right thing—I wanted to keep Helen safe.

LISA: Well, you shouldn't have been so bloody *thoughtful!*

DANIEL: [*reeling*] I never knew you were mad about this.

LISA: Neither did I…

> *It's a revelation. Her face is streaked with tears.* DANIEL *reaches into his knapsack and pulls out a hankie, handing it to her.*

DANIEL: Here…

LISA: Thanks. Is this dirty?

DANIEL: [*smiling*] It's clean, I promise.

> LISA *blows her nose loudly.*

LISA: You know what I wish? I wish your beautiful, thick, brown hair was going grey or falling out. That'd be the most beautiful sight in the world to me: you with wrinkles around your eyes and sun spots starting to appear on your hands and a saggy, middle-aged gut—

DANIEL: Fuck!

LISA: It's true, I'd love it… I'm sorry I hit you.

DANIEL: I forgive you.

> *He pretends to punch her back and then pulls her into a hug. This time she allows it. They hold each other in silence for a beat or two, then:*

LISA: Dan. I've always wondered… when you woke up on that Friday, how did you feel?

DANIEL: What do you mean?

LISA: Well, did you feel weird? Or strange?

DANIEL: I just felt hungry. We didn't have any bread for toast—it was Stevo's turn to do the shop.

LISA: So you didn't have any sense of foreboding? No bad feeling?

DANIEL: Nope.

LISA: Really? Nothing at all?

DANIEL: Actually, I woke up and I thought, 'I'd better wear my best undies today, they'll be scraping me off the road tonight'.

LISA: Dan!

DANIEL: Well, it's like that's what you want me to say. It was just another day, Lise.

LISA: I just thought you *must* have had a feeling?

DANIEL: I'm glad I didn't. How could you get through a day if you knew you'd be dead at the end of it?

LISA: But maybe if you'd had a feeling you wouldn't have given away your helmet?

DANIEL: You've got to stop stressing about the helmet—it's not like I planned it, Lise. Helen's mum was going to pick her up, but her car broke down. She only lived two k's away, so it seemed like a piece of cake—and I *wanted* her to have the helmet. I liked her. I was trying to be romantic.

LISA: Well, it worked. There was a story in the paper three days later: 'Bike Crash Girl Saved By Love'.

DANIEL: Yeah? That's pretty cool.

LISA: I thought so at first.

DANIEL: Did you write it?

LISA: Me? Three days after you died? I could barely write my name.

DANIEL: What page was it on?

LISA: I don't know, somewhere near the front.

DANIEL: Page three?

LISA: I can't remember.

DANIEL: Was it big? Did it have a picture of me?

LISA: Dan, I don't care! All *I* remember is meeting Helen: 'This is your brother's new girlfriend; she's got a sprained wrist because she was wearing the only helmet. And here's your twin: he's the body on the slab.'

DANIEL: Shit. Lise.

LISA: Well, that's how it was. Can you imagine if that had been me?

DANIEL: Fuck. Don't do that to me.

LISA: Why not? You did it to me.

DANIEL: I'm sorry, it's all so stuffed… but I can't go back and change what I did… and if I hadn't given her the helmet, *she'd* be dead.

LISA: Have you ever heard of two helmets?

DANIEL: I'm sorry.

LISA: [*a revelation*] You know what, Dan? You're always saying how unlucky you are, but two people on a bike with only one helmet—that had nothing to do with bad luck, it was a bad *decision*.

DANIEL: It was a bad decision followed by bad luck.

LISA: Yeah—but if you'd made a *good* decision, the bad luck wouldn't have killed you. Do you have any idea what you put us all through? It was horrendous... the whole family was walking around like zombies... and even though it was their loss too, I felt completely alone.

DANIEL: [*taking her hand*] Lise...

LISA: It was just so wrong... We were this big together, the size of a speck on a fingernail, and we grew in the womb together, so surely we should be in the same coffin?

DANIEL: You've got to stop doing this to yourself...

LISA: You know what else I've always wanted to know? What was your last conversation about?

DANIEL: My last conversation?

LISA: Yeah, your final words. What were you saying in the seconds just before?

DANIEL: Nothing. Who can talk on a motorbike?

LISA: Well, what were you thinking?

DANIEL: I don't know. I just remember that— No, you don't want to hear this.

LISA: Yes I do. Tell me.

DANIEL: Well... I was coming up to the intersection, but there was this big bush thing on the corner. I couldn't see anyone coming—

LISA: I know. The Falcon couldn't see you either. The coroner said it was nobody's fault... that kind of makes it worse. Go on.

DANIEL: Are you sure? Well... we were just into the intersection and Helen suddenly screamed. And then I saw him coming, and I put my foot down but my bike was too gutless—

LISA: Okay—stop.

DANIEL: But before we left home we were talking about Alexis Carrington Colby.

LISA: Alexis Carrington Colby *Dexter*.

DANIEL: Dexter?

LISA: Yeah. She must have married Dex Dexter after you died... that's really all you were talking about? 'Dynasty'?

DANIEL: It was just stupid stuff. I'm sorry, Lise. I should have lied and said we were discussing the meaning of life.

LISA: That was a Monty Python movie: *The Meaning of Life*.

DANIEL: Yeah?

LISA: Yeah, it must have been just after your time.

DANIEL: Was it as funny as *Life of Brian*? I killed myself laughing in that movie.

He lights a cigarette.

LISA: Not another one?

DANIEL: Why are you always judging me lately? Can't I have one small pleasure?

LISA: But do you have to have forty 'small pleasures' a day? The fags would've killed you if the crash hadn't done it first—and that would've been self-inflicted too.

DANIEL: We've already established that I'm a loser, so why don't you just leave me to it?

LISA: I've never said you were a loser—

DANIEL: You didn't have to, it's obvious—

LISA: That's ridiculous—

DANIEL: I don't even know why you bother to try. You know I'll always do the wrong thing—

LISA: [*flaring*] Well, isn't that convenient? Poor, underestimated Dan. Why take responsibility for your actions when you can fall back on that victim crap?

DANIEL *stares at her, distressed and confused.*

DANIEL: What's happening, Lise? I feel like since you've met that old guy you're starting to hate me.

LISA: Don't say that.

DANIEL: Why not? I reckon it's true. You're changing.

LISA: I'm sorry. I don't hate you… I love you so much… but I'm scared I'm losing my grip on you.

DANIEL: No you're not.

He playfully grips her.

I'm right here, aren't I?

LISA: Are you? Really? I don't know anymore. What if you're a figment of my imagination? Or a manifestation of my subconscious?

DANIEL: A what of your what?

> *But* LISA's *not laughing.*

LISA: Dan, I'm worried… I can't seem to keep the world away.

DANIEL: Yes, you can.

LISA: No, I can't. Not anymore. We're in danger and I don't know what to do—*you'll* have to save us.

DANIEL: [*panicking*] Me? But, Lise—

> *He takes a step towards her but his legs crumple beneath him and he falls to the floor. She hurries to him.*

LISA: Are you okay?

DANIEL: [*shaken*] I'm cool…

> *He tries to stand and falls again.*

Shit.

LISA: [*panicking*] Dan, what are you doing?

> *She helps him up.*

Get up! Come on, stand up! You have to save us—

DANIEL: How can *I* save us? I haven't 'crossed to the other side' and turned into some kind of saint. I'm just a punk—

LISA: You're not a punk—

DANIEL: I'm just a guy who did something dumb and died.

LISA: But that's not fair. All young guys do stupid things, but they don't all die—why did *you*?

DANIEL: Fucked if I know.

> LISA *releases her hold on him and he falls again.*

LISA: No! Dan, get up!

> *She helps him up.*

Please don't do this—*I'm* out of options. We can only survive if it's your decision—

DANIEL: Then we're stuffed. We both know I made my last decision when I drove into that intersection.

> LISA *feels a rush of terror.*

LISA: Dan. You have to save us!

DANIEL: [*losing his temper*] I can't fucking save us! I rode a bike without a helmet, I never made it to our twenty-first—so don't try and make me into something I'm not. Don't put that on me, it's not fucking fair.

Lights out...

Fade up the raucous intro into Stiff Little Fingers' '(Don't Want To Be) Nobody's Hero' (1981)...

◊ ◊ ◊

A spotlight appears and DANIEL *jumps up and down, dancing beneath it, completely immersed in the raw energy of the song.*

But as the vocals kick in and Jake Burns snarls about needy fans putting him up on a pedestal, DANIEL *crumples at the knees and falls. He picks himself up and tries to dance again, but he keeps falling over.*

As the lights and music fade DANIEL *is on the floor, struggling to get back onto his feet...*

◊ ◊ ◊

A spotlight fades up on a tombstone:
Daniel James Fitzgerald
18.09.62–30.10.82

LISA *is sitting on Daniel's grave arranging flowers in a vase beside the headstone.*

TOM *appears behind her, en route back to his car. He stops in surprise when he sees her. As he hesitates, not sure whether to say hello, she turns and sees him.*

LISA: Oh... Tom. Hi...
TOM: Hi... I've just been... [*Gesturing*] My dad's over there.
LISA: I wondered if he was here...

A beat as he silently asks the obvious question.

This is my twin brother. Dan.
TOM: Your twin? You never said...
LISA: I know.
TOM: [*looking at the tombstone*] It's his birthday... That must make it yours. Happy birthday.
LISA: Thanks. If you'd like to hang around, we'll be cutting the cake in a few minutes.

They both laugh a little. What can they say?

How's your dad today?

TOM: Situation unchanged. [*Reading*] Daniel James…

LISA: Yeah. He's fifteen minutes older than me… I mean, he *was*. I thought if I came here and looked at this [*the headstone*] for long enough, I might finally convince myself that he's dead.

TOM: [*reading*] October 30, 1982.

LISA: It was six weeks after we turned twenty. So long ago—get over it, right?

TOM: I'd never say something that stupid.

LISA: It *is* stupid, isn't it? 'Are you over it yet?' As if. You don't get over it, you get used to it—or you *try* to.

TOM: You're not there yet?

LISA: I think I've still got a few 'issues'—not that you would have noticed.

   TOM *can't help smiling.*

Tom. I'm sorry I've been such a monumental dickhead.

TOM: You *have* been a monumental dickhead.

LISA: I know. If it's any consolation, I've only been a monumental dickhead because I like you… monumentally.

   TOM *looks pleased but wary.*

Your honesty's rubbing off on me.

   They smile at each other.

TOM: Do you come here every birthday?

LISA: No. Actually, I haven't been here since soon after he died. My parents and sisters and my younger brother come, so I know this [*the grave*] is well looked after, but for me…

TOM: Too hard?

LISA: I can remember sitting on this spot about eight months after he died, and it was like I could feel him rotting underneath me. All I could think of were the maggots and bugs that were eating his beautiful face away. I couldn't eat. I couldn't sleep. Every time I closed my eyes I saw him lying under the ground with his flesh collapsing away from his bones and ants and worms swarming all over him, carrying bits of him away, like his cute dimples, or his beautiful long eyelashes… Sorry. You don't want to hear this stuff.

TOM: I'm listening, aren't I? So you've stayed away?

LISA: I didn't want to think of him like that. I wanted to remember him how he was—but I think I remember him a bit *too well*... Can I tell you something I've never told anyone? Even now, I still feel like he's here. I can still see him so clearly—I still talk to him every day. And I know it's not logical, but being happy with somebody else... it's felt like a betrayal. It's a totally different love, but still... I must sound like an idiot.

TOM: No, actually you're finally making some sense.

LISA: I really am sorry for stuffing you around. You've had a crappy year, and I've hardly helped.

TOM: Yeah... but I'm a glutton for punishment.

> *He's smiling. Could this mean he'll give her another chance?*

Colonel Klink's in the car. Would you like to meet him?

LISA: I'd love to.

TOM: Okay, but I should warn you—he's still vulnerable from the marriage break-up. So, if there's any chance you'll suddenly jump out of the car, or try and talk to him about tax, I don't think you should make his acquaintance... What do you think?

> *He waits.*

LISA: Tom. Can you promise me that you won't die? That I'll never get a call or a knock at the door?

TOM: Of course I can't. Can you promise me?

LISA: But I'm scared...

TOM: We're all scared.

LISA: I'm *more* scared.

TOM: Okay, you win.

> LISA *laughs.*

It's your call. What do you say?

> LISA *is silent as she wages a final internal battle with the fear that's crippled her for so long. Then:*

LISA: I'd love to meet Colonel Klink.

TOM: Great. Want a hand with those creaky old knees?

> *He helps her up to her feet. They walk off hand-in-hand.*

Lights fade…

In the darkness we fade up the first verse of the acoustic version of 'Almost with You' by The Church from the Liberation Blue Acoustic Series *album (various artists, 2007)…*

◊ ◊ ◊

Lights up. LISA *walks into Daniel's bedroom.*

DANIEL*'s lying asleep, curled up in the foetal position.*

LISA *moves to the bed and lies down behind him. She curls herself into him just as she imagines they were in the womb. The lighting state changes to intimate that they're floating in a liquid womb together…*

As they lie, curled up 'in-utero', 'Almost with You' fades up into its bittersweet chorus…

DANIEL *stirs. He's surprised to see* LISA *curled up so close. He grins sleepily.*

DANIEL: Hey, you're invading my personal space, you stalker.
LISA: Dan. You have to go.
DANIEL: I know…

> *He turns to face her and they hug each other tight for a long moment.*

I love you, Lise.
LISA: I love you too.

> *They climb off the bed, taking one another's hand.*

> *The lighting state changes as they walk to downstage centre and look out to the audience, hand-in-hand.*

This is my twin. He's twenty years old.
DANIEL: This is my twin. She's forty-five. In ten years time she'll be 55 and I still won't have any wrinkles.
LISA: My eternally beautiful brother.

> *They kiss each other on the cheek in farewell.*

DANIEL: Be happy, Lise.

> *She nods. The lights dim softly as* DANIEL *slowly lets go of* LISA*'s outstretched hand and melts away into the darkness…*

LISA *stands alone for several seconds, then the lights dim and we fade up Simple Minds' 'Don't You Forget About Me' (1982) for the curtain call.*

THE END

In memory of Gregory Daniel Coleman
25.09.62 – 05.11.82

www.ingramcontent.com/pod-product-compliance
Lightning Source LLC
Chambersburg PA
CBHW050025090426
42734CB00021B/3418